GW00686308

THIS BOOK BELONGS TO

————————————————————

13-Digit ISBN: 978-1604337020
10-Digit ISBN: 1604337028

This book may be ordered by mail from the publisher. Please include $5.99 for
postage and handling. Please support your local bookseller first!

Books published by Cider Mill Press Book Publishers are available at special
discounts for bulk purchases in the United States by corporations, institutions, and
other organizations. For more information, please contact the publisher.

Cider Mill Press Book Publishers
Where good books are ready for press
PO Box 454
12 Spring Street
Kennebunkport, Maine 04046
Visit us on the Web! www.cidermillpress.com

Design by Alicia Freile, Tango Media
Typography: Bauer Bodoni, Georgia, AT Sackers Gothic
and Adobe Woodtype Ornaments

Image Credits: Front endpapers: John F. Kennedy home, Brookline, MA, Carol
M. Highsmith (Library of Congress, LC-HS503- 695); Lt. John F. Kennedy 1942,
Frank Turgeon, Jr.; Ticker tape parade, Burton Berinsky; back endpapers: Jackie
Bouvier Kennedy and John F. Kennedy cutting the cake at their wedding, Sept.
12, 1953, Newport, RI, Toni Frissell (Library of Congress, LC-HS503- 4801) and
Hammersmith Farm, the "Summer White House" from 1961 to 1963, Carol M.
Highsmith (Library of Congress, LC-F9-04-5309-09 -07); all other images, John F.
Kennedy Presidential Library and Museum.

Printed in China
1 2 3 4 5 6 7 8 9 0
First Edition

JOHN F. KENNEDY

NOTEBOOK

CIDER MILL PRESS

BOOK PUBLISHERS

Kennebunkport, Maine

John F. Kennedy:
The Power behind His Prose

By Mim Harrison

When John F. Kennedy was preparing his Inaugural Address for January 20, 1961, he wanted it to be short (it was—just 1,347 words) and to have as few references to himself as possible. A concordance of key words in the address shows only four uses of *I*; among the words that sounded the trumpet most frequently were *we* and *us, free* and *world, America, pledge, ask.* They were words intended to resonate, and they did.

Kennedy's Inaugural Address ranks among America's leading speeches. It is not the only speech by Kennedy making such a list—perhaps because a better word than "speech" is "oratory."

Kennedy had an ear for language, which is why even when simply reading a quotation by him,

v

we hear it. He was an ardent admirer of Winston Churchill, another great orator of his century. As the son of the U.S. Ambassador to Great Britain, Kennedy was in Parliament in 1939 when Winston Churchill declaimed on Britain's moral imperative to crush Hitler. Years later, as Kennedy campaigned for the presidency, he would listen to recordings of Churchill's speeches.

Lincoln was another great inspiration, his Gettysburg Address—astonishingly short for the time—among the speeches Kennedy admired. The cadence of Lincoln and Churchill are at times echoed in Kennedy's, who also knew the value of such literary underpinnings as alliterations ("pay any price, bear any burden") and chiasmus ("Let us never negotiate out of fear. But let us never fear to negotiate.").

But Kennedy's genius for the memorable phrase lies deeper than these literary devices. Like both Churchill and Lincoln, Kennedy was a voracious reader. He took an ecumenical approach to citing great works in his own. He would quote from both ancient and contemporary sources, from the Bible and Chinese proverbs, Aristotle and Socrates, Rousseau and Emerson, Hemingway, and even Oscar Wilde.

He also enjoyed poetry, particularly that of Lord Byron and, of course, Robert Frost, who recited at the Inauguration. Evelyn Lincoln, Kennedy's secretary, listed "Ulysses" by Alfred, Lord Tennyson, as his favorite.

As early as his Harvard days, Kennedy compiled in notebooks passages he admired, those by Thomas Paine and Thomas Jefferson being but two. He would also scribble quotes on the fly on scraps of paper, to be added later to his notebooks. (Lincoln had a similar habit, capturing thoughts and phrases that came into his head on scraps of paper that he then tossed into his hat—that sartorial element that met its demise with Kennedy.)

"Scribble" is particularly apt in Kennedy's case. His handwriting was a muddle—the direct opposite of his lapidary prose, and his extraordinarily quick mind.

Kennedy's delivery of his Inaugural Address exemplifies another reason why his writing is so compelling: he was constantly editing himself.

Although the reading copy of the Inaugural Address has not one scribble on its fourteen pages, Kennedy actually made more than thirty changes to the text as he delivered it. One of them was to the most iconic sentence of the speech.

"...ask not what your country will do for you..." is how the first clause of that sentence *read*. "...ask not what your country can do for you..." is what Kennedy actually *spoke*, instantly creating a powerful parallel with the "can" in the second clause: "...ask what you can do for your country."

For all of his eloquence, though, the power of his language lay even deeper. As his close adviser Theodore Sorensen observed, Kennedy "moved people not because of the grandeur of his phrases... but because of the grandeur of his ideas." And he moved people to act. Among those who answered the call to ask what they could do for their country was the Pulitzer Prize-winning historian David McCullough.

"To strive, to seek, to find..." reads a portion of the last line of Tennyson's "Ulysses." Kennedy's words encourage us to strive, and to seek. His lofty rhetoric invites us to aspire to similar heights. Through his words, John F. Kennedy elevates us.

Mim Harrison is the editor of *John F. Kennedy: The Making of His Inaugural Address*. She has also edited and produced books on two leaders that President Kennedy admired, Winston Churchill and Abraham Lincoln. The latter includes *Long Remembered: Lincoln and His Five Versions of the Gettysburg Address*, in cooperation with the Library of Congress.

Handwritten notes from President Kennedy's Inaugural Address

ask not

What your country is going to do
for you — Ask what you can do
for your country — my fellow
citizens of the world — ask not
                    or others
what America will do for you —
                      give you
ask rather what you can do
for freedom. Work of yours —

the same high standards of
price and strength of heart
and will they wish for
you. ~~That~~ alliance for
~~... progress~~ will be for good

President John F. Kennedy delivering the Inaugural Address,
Washington, D.C., January 20, 1961

And so, my fellow Americans: **ASK NOT WHAT YOUR COUNTRY** can do for you — ask what you can do for your country. My fellow citizens of the world: **ASK NOT WHAT AMERICA** will do for you, but what together we can do for the freedom of man.

– INAUGURAL ADDRESS (JANUARY 20, 1961)

Man is still the most
EXTRAORDINARY
computer of all.

– REMARKS UPON PRESENTING THE NASA
DISTINGUISHED SERVICE MEDAL TO ASTRONAUT
L. GORDON COOPER (MAY 21, 1963)

*President Kennedy and astronaut John Glenn look inside
the Freedom 7 space capsule February 23, 1962*

Children are the world's **MOST VALUABLE RESOURCE** and its best hope for the future.

—UNICEF APPEAL
(JULY 25, 1963)

President John F. Kennedy, Caroline Kennedy, John F. Kennedy, Jr., and Macaroni the Pony at the White House, June 22, 1962

The problems of the world cannot possibly be solved by skeptics or cynics whose horizons are limited by the obvious realities. **WE NEED MEN WHO CAN DREAM OF THINGS THAT NEVER WERE...** and ask why not.

–ADDRESS BEFORE THE IRISH PARLIAMENT IN DUBLIN (JUNE 28, 1963)

President and Mrs. Kennedy in Hyannis Port with Caroline,
John Jr., and family dogs, August 14, 1963

Let us welcome
controversial
BOOKS and
controversial
AUTHORS.

—*SATURDAY REVIEW* (OCTOBER 29, 1960)

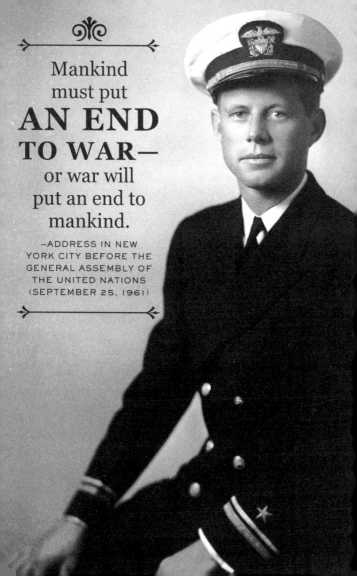

Mankind
must put
**AN END
TO WAR—**
or war will
put an end to
mankind.

—ADDRESS IN NEW
YORK CITY BEFORE THE
GENERAL ASSEMBLY OF
THE UNITED NATIONS
(SEPTEMBER 25, 1961)

Lt. John F. Kennedy, 1942
Photo: Frank Turgeon, Jr.

If a free society cannot
HELP THE MANY
who are poor, it cannot save
the few who are rich.

—INAUGURAL ADDRESS (JANUARY 20, 1961)

Let us think of education as the means
of developing our greatest abilities,
because in each of us there is a

PRIVATE HOPE AND DREAM

which, fulfilled, can be translated into
benefit for everyone and greater
strength for our nation.

—PROCLAMATION 3422—AMERICAN EDUCATION
WEEK, 1961 (JULY 25, 1961)

*President Kennedy poses with members of the younger generation
of Kennedys, Hyannis Port, Massachusetts, August 3, 1963*

All this will not be finished in the first one hundred days. Nor will it be finished in the first one thousand days, nor in the life of this administration, nor even perhaps in our lifetime on this planet.

BUT LET US BEGIN.

—INAUGURAL ADDRESS (JANUARY 20, 1961)

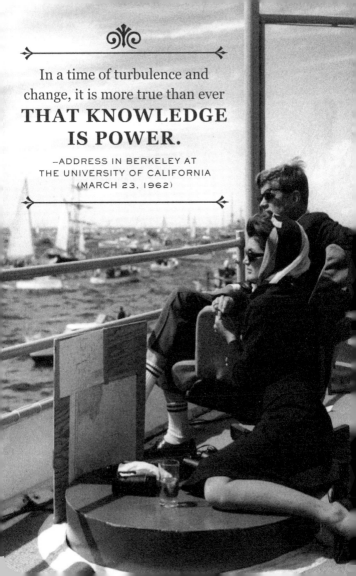

In a time of turbulence and change, it is more true than ever

THAT KNOWLEDGE IS POWER.

—ADDRESS IN BERKELEY AT
THE UNIVERSITY OF CALIFORNIA
(MARCH 23, 1962)

President John F. Kennedy and First Lady Jacqueline Kennedy
watch the first race of the 1962 America's Cup from aboard
the USS Joseph P. Kennedy, *September 15, 1962,*
Newport, Rhode Island

President and Mrs. Kennedy greet Fredric March,
Nobel Prize winner, April 29, 1962

We must never forget that **ART IS NOT** a form of propaganda; it is **A FORM OF TRUTH.**

—REMARKS AT AMHERST COLLEGE UPON
RECEIVING AN HONORARY DEGREE
(OCTOBER 12, 1963)

We are tied
TO THE OCEAN.
And when we go back
to the sea, whether it is
to sail or to watch it,
we are going back from
whence we came.

—REMARKS IN NEWPORT AT THE AUSTRALIAN
AMBASSADOR'S DINNER FOR THE AMERICA'S CUP
CREWS (SEPTEMBER 14, 1962)

President Kennedy aboard the U.S. Coast Guard yacht
Manitou, *Maine, August 11, 1962*

We choose to go to the moon in this decade and do the other things, not because they are easy but because **THEY ARE HARD,** because that goal will serve to organize and measure the best of our energies and skills, because that challenge is one that we are willing to accept, one we are **UNWILLING TO POSTPONE**, and one which **WE INTEND TO WIN.**

–ADDRESS AT RICE UNIVERSITY IN HOUSTON
ON THE NATION'S SPACE EFFORT
(SEPTEMBER 12, 1962)

We celebrate the past to awaken the future.

—SPEECH BY SENATOR JOHN F. KENNEDY,
MEMORIAL PROGRAM, 25TH ANNIVERSARY
OF SIGNING OF SOCIAL SECURITY ACT,
HYDE PARK, NY (AUGUST 14, 1960)

President Kennedy with Caroline aboard the "Honey Fitz,"
August 25, 1963

The Constitution makes us
not rivals for power
BUT PARTNERS
FOR PROGRESS.

—ANNUAL MESSAGE TO THE CONGRESS ON THE
STATE OF THE UNION (JANUARY 11, 1962)

*President and Mrs. Kennedy arrive for the First Inaugural
Salute to the President Dinner, National Guard Armory,
January 20, 1962*

I want to emphasize in
the great concentration
which we now place upon
scientists and engineers how
much we still need the
**MEN AND WOMEN
EDUCATED IN THE
LIBERAL TRADITION**,
willing to take the long look,
undisturbed by prejudices
and slogans of the moment,
who attempt to make
an honest judgment on
difficult events.

–ADDRESS AT THE UNIVERSITY OF NORTH
CAROLINA UPON RECEIVING AN HONORARY
DEGREE (OCTOBER 10, 1961)

So let us begin anew—
remembering on both sides that
civility is not a sign of weakness, and
sincerity is always subject to proof.

LET US NEVER
NEGOTIATE
OUT OF FEAR.

But let us never fear to negotiate.

–INAUGURAL ADDRESS (JANUARY 20, 1961)

Great crises produce great men, and great
DEEDS OF COURAGE.

– PROFILES IN COURAGE, 1956

*President Kennedy with representative cadets of service
academies, January 29, 1961*

The world is very
different now.
**FOR MAN
HOLDS IN HIS
MORTAL HANDS
THE POWER**
to abolish all forms
of human poverty,
and all forms of
human life.

—INAUGURAL ADDRESS (JANUARY 20, 1961)

President and Mrs. Kennedy with Caroline and John Jr.,
Hyannis Port, MA August 4, 1962

The Chinese use two brush strokes
to write the word "crisis." One brush
stroke stands for danger;
the other for opportunity.

IN A CRISIS, BE AWARE OF THE DANGER— BUT RECOGNIZE THE OPPORTUNITY.

–CAMPAIGN SPEECH BY SENATOR JOHN F.
KENNEDY (INDIANAPOLIS, APRIL 12, 1959, AND
VALLEY FORGE, OCTOBER 29, 1960)

John F. Kennedy campaigning at a Wall Street ticker tape parade, October 19, 1960

For, in the final analysis,
our most basic common link
is that we all inhabit this
small planet. We all breathe
the same air. We all cherish
our children's future.
And we are all mortal.

—COMMENCEMENT ADDRESS AT
AMERICAN UNIVERSITY IN WASHINGTON
(JUNE 10, 1963)